THE BOOK OF FANTASTIC
INSECTS

Illustrated by
PETER BARRETT

Written by
JANE CARRUTH

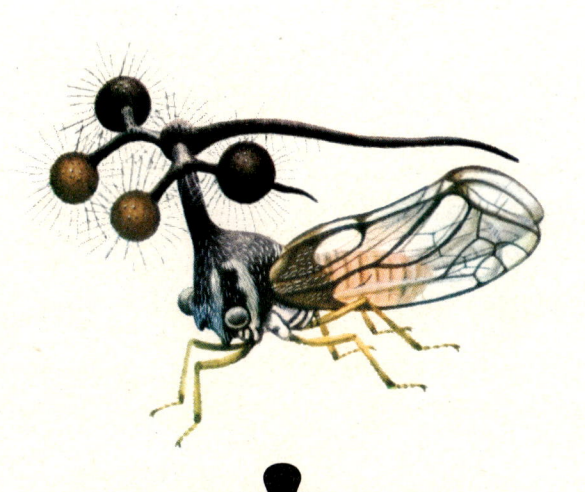

octopus

CONTENTS

Ichneumon Wasp
European Hornet
Leaf Beetle
Tropical Flower Beetle
Giraffe Stag Beetle
Sun Dung Beetle
Hercules Beetle
Weevil
Lantern Fly
Leaf Insect
Common Stick Insect
Walkingstick
Death's Head Cicada
Croesus Moth
Windowpane Butterfly
Death's Head Hawk Moth
Treehoppers
Waxen-tailed Planthopper
Leaf-footed Bug
Mantis
Mantis
False Leaf Bush Cricket
Mole-Cricket
Grasshopper

INTRODUCTION

All insects, no matter whether they hop, run or fly, have one thing in common. They have bodies that are in three parts: a head with a pair of feelers or antennae, a thorax with three pairs of legs, and an abdomen.

Today there are many more insects in the world than there are other animals. Entomologists (men who study insects) are already aware of nearly a million different species and they are discovering new kinds every year. This diversity of insect life is fascinating. Some insects have wings and others are wingless. Some can sing, while others have no voice at all. A butterfly always has little knobs on its antennae, while moths never do. A beetle cannot grow any bigger after it becomes an adult, no matter how much food it eats.

Insects have been on the earth for at least 200 million years and, with their tremendous capacity for survival, they have outlived all the giant beasts of prehistoric times whose species have vanished from the face of our planet. Millions and millions of years ago, there were grasshoppers and crickets and beetles just as there are today. Some of these prehistoric insects were attracted to a golden, sticky resin that fell from trees long ago. The resin trapped the insects and, through the ages, this resin hardened into stone, leaving fossilized grasshoppers and crickets that are often displayed in today's museums.

This book contains some of the world's most interesting insects. It begins with two fearsome-looking insects, the Wasp and the Hornet. Several members of the beetle family follow next, including the long-nosed Weevil; and then the Lantern Fly, whose long nose looks like the jaws of a crocodile, is shown. Following three of nature's best mimics, the Leaf, Stick and Walkingstick Insects, several moths and butterflies are shown. The Planthopper, Leaf-footed Bug, and Mantis are also described. And the book ends with the well-disguised False Leaf Bush Cricket, the Mole Cricket, and finally the familiar Grasshopper.

Some words that may be unfamiliar are explained in the glossary at the back of this book.

ICHNEUMON WASP

Habitat: Pine forests, mainly in Europe. **Size** 1¼ in.
It can drill through wood.

The wasp you see here is one of the biggest members of the Ichneumon Wasp family. All the female members of this family carry out a strangely parasitic practise when laying their eggs. The female, shown here, flies around, using her sensitive antennae to search out a tree that is the home of a wood-wasp larva. With her long, sharp ovipositor she drills a hole in the wood and lays an egg on this larva. When her own larva develops it will feed on the larva of the wood-wasp, which, as a result, dies of starvation. Foresters welcome the Ichneumon Wasp, for there is no more deadly enemy to the life and growth of a tree than the destructive wood-wasp.

EUROPEAN HORNET

Habitat: Europe. **Size:** 1 in.
It is one of the most ferocious insects.

At close range and magnified many times, this Hornet, found all over Europe, looks terrifyingly business-like. And its business is terrifying! For it is one of the fiercest predators in the insect kingdom. Not only does the Hornet pursue and demolish other insects to satisfy its own enormous appetite, but it feeds its larva on their remains. It is often the case in the insect world that the female is more menacing than the male. In the case of the hornet, it is the female that stings, and if you have ever been stung by one, you know how painful it can be. Anyone unfortunate enough to disturb a hornet's nest would almost certainly require medical attention. This particular Hornet often inhabits the same nest year after year. The queen hibernates throughout the winter and founds her new colony in the spring, when a single colony may have as many as 5,000 inmates!

LEAF BEETLE

Habitat: Australia and Asia. **Size:** 1 in.
It jumps like a kangaroo.

There are more beetles in the insect kingdom than hornets and wasps put together. And there are a vast number of different species. But it is easy to recognise a beetle, no matter what kind, from the horny, shell-like covering that is formed out of its forewings. Like butterflies and moths they lay eggs, and their grubs are often far more destructive than the beetles themselves.

Some species of beetle live in water, others in soil or sand. Others again, like the Leaf Beetle of Australia and Asia, that you see here, are found among plants.

With its frog-like legs and remarkable jumping ability it is often known as the Kangaroo Beetle. Although beautifully coloured, the Leaf Beetle causes considerable damage to the flowers and plants which are its chief source of food.

TROPICAL FLOWER BEETLE

Habitat: West Africa.
Size: body 1½–2½ in. long, nose projection ½ in. long.
It is one of the most beautiful beetles.

This pretty Tropical Flower Beetle, with its distinctive colouring, is found in West Africa, where it is collected by the natives as an object of beauty like a jewel. Illustrated here, the male of this particular species is distinguished by its odd snout-like nose. The beautifully marked forewings that meet down the centre of its back protect large fragile hind wings that the beetle uses for flying. Nearly all beetles can fly, and to do so they lift up their forewings and then use their hind wings like a moth or butterfly.

GIRAFFE STAG BEETLE

Habitat: Mostly tropics. **Size:** 3¾ in.
It has 'antlers' like a stag.

There are nearly a thousand different kinds of Stag Beetle. Some, like the Giraffe Stag Beetle, have spectacular mandibles that are almost as long as their bodies. These impressive 'jaws' are used for crushing food and for fighting, mostly with other Stag Beetles. To look at they are not unlike the antlers of a stag, making it easy to see how Stag Beetles get their name.

The female Stag Beetle lays her eggs in decaying trees. The six years it may then take the larvae of some of the big Stag Beetles to reach the adult stage are very important. The size and strength of a grown Stag Beetle depends entirely on the quality of food it has eaten during its larval stage.

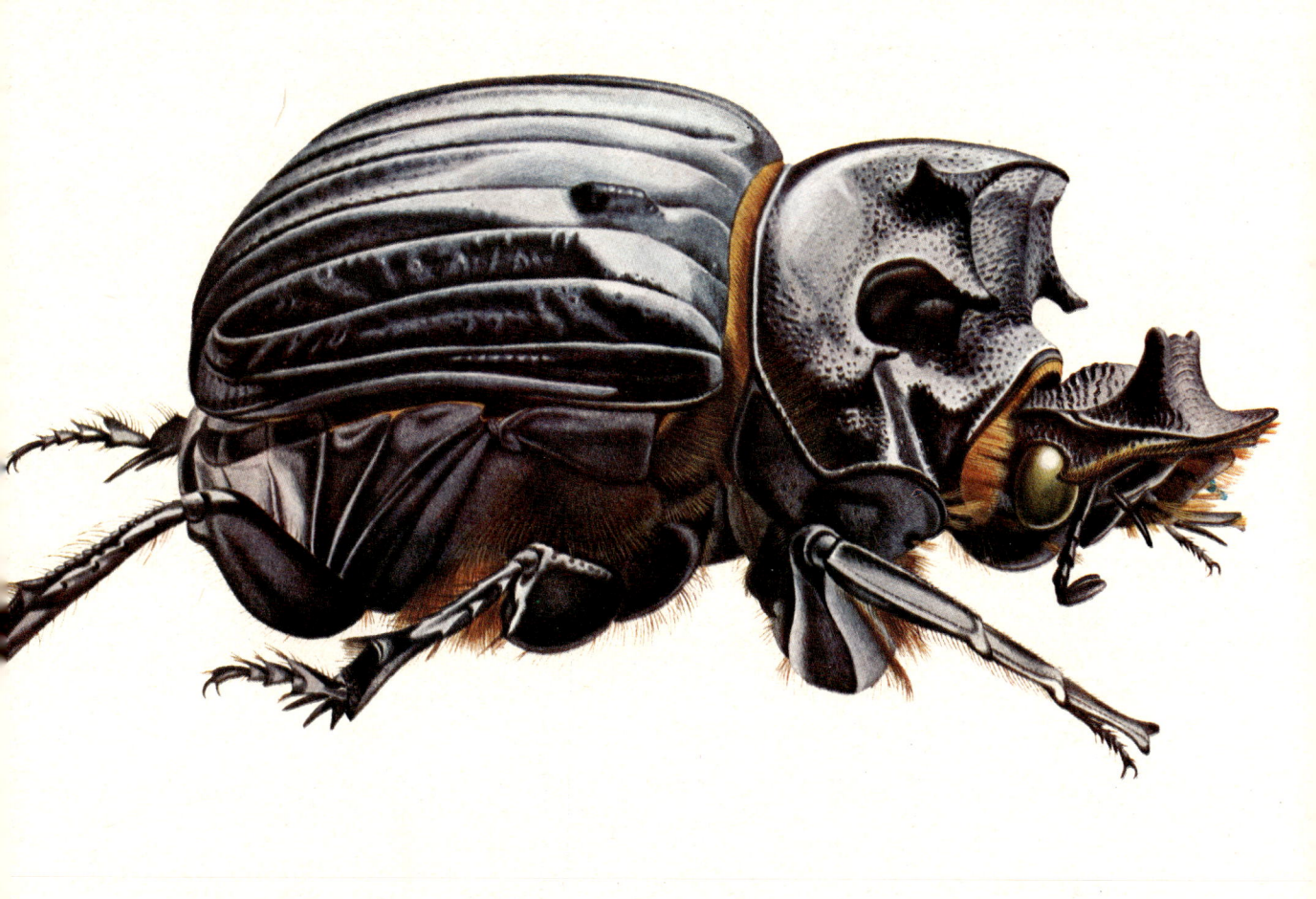

SUN DUNG BEETLE

Habitat: World-wide. **Size:** 2½ in.
It is a ball-roller.

The sturdy little Sun Dung Beetle belongs to the Scarab Beetle family. These energetic beetles spend most of their time searching out fresh manure which they shape into a round, compact ball and push along with their front legs. If they are working in pairs, the second beetle may turn itself about and assist in the pushing with its hind legs.
Then these extraordinary beetles burrow into the earth until they have dug a tunnel deep enough to hold their 'ball'. The beetles will then live underground for just as long as their food supply lasts. When the manure is finished, they set off again to replenish their store-cupboard. Later in the year, the female fusses around until she finds really fresh manure to make a ball in which she can deposit her egg. She places her egg in a small opening in the ball, and then hides it away underground. When the grub appears it feeds on the manure until it is ready to push its way out, and the new young beetle then takes up the ball-rolling occupation of its parents.

HERCULES BEETLE

Habitat: Central and South America. **Size:** 6 in.
It is the longest beetle in the world.

Strange as it may seem, the Hercules Beetle of the Central and South American tropical jungles belongs to the same family as the dung-pushing beetles. It also has several rare and unusual relatives like the Rhinoceros Beetle that, with its unique arrangement of horns, looks rather like a tiny rhinoceros, and the big Elephant Beetle of Australia. Both the Hercules Beetle and the Rhinoceros Beetle are highly prized by collectors.
In the record books, the Hercules Beetle gains recognition for being the longest beetle in the world! Fearsome to look at, the male has two fantastically long, toothed horns, as you can see from the picture. Nearly two-thirds of this six-inch beetle is, in fact, accounted for by its horn. As with so many insects, the female has no claim to distinction, for instead of an outlandish horn all she has is an inconspicuous knob.
Named, because of its great strength, after Hercules, a hero of Greek mythology, this huge beetle is among the most frightening of all in the insect world.

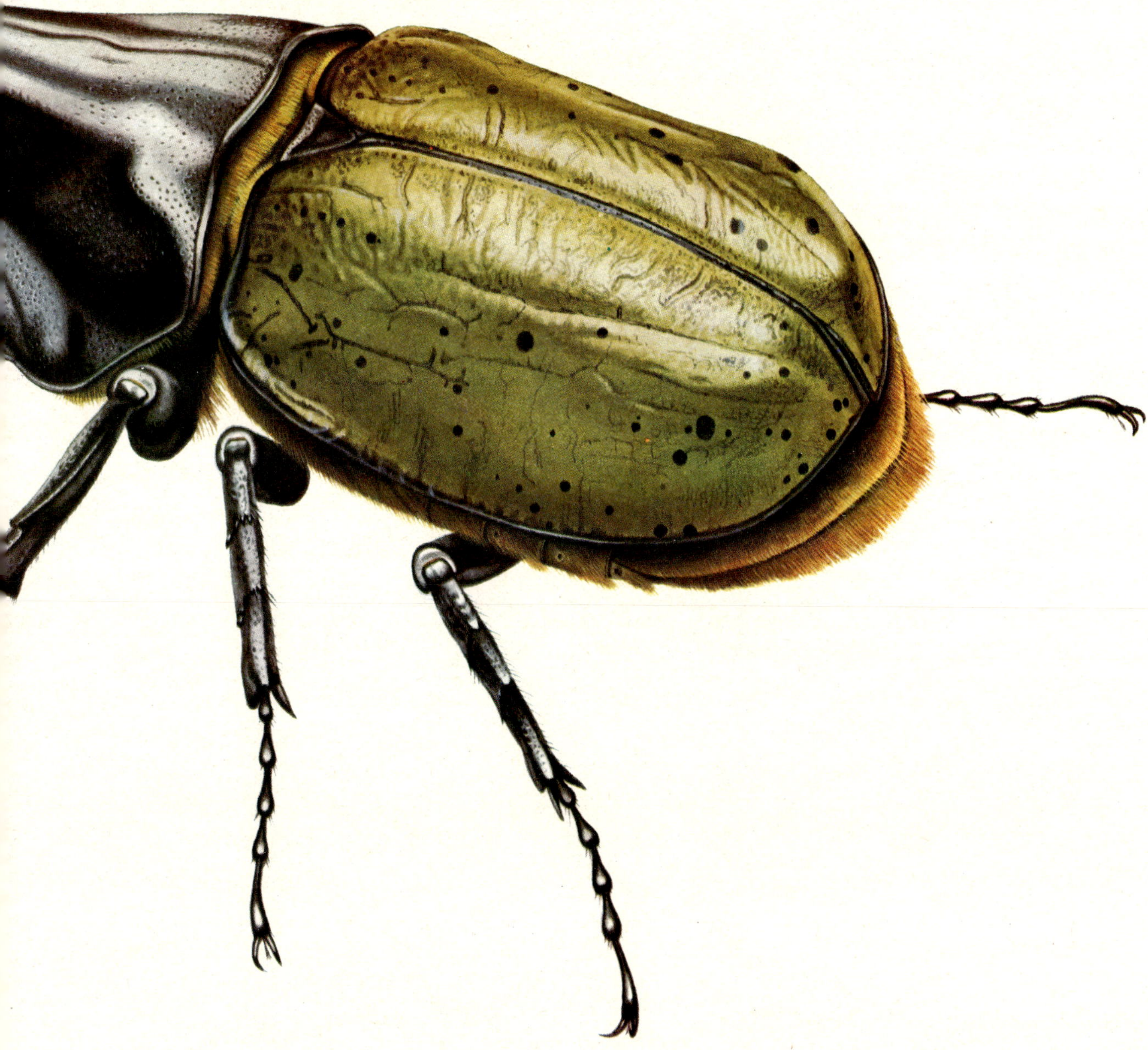

WEEVIL

Habitat: World-wide. **Size:** 3 in.
It has an amazingly long nose.

In sharp contrast to the heavyweight beetles are the slim-line weevils, members of the Brenthid Beetle family. Weevils are quite unlike other beetles for their heads are shaped like snouts with the mouth at the end. They have antennae that are elbowed, and are active and destructive insects.

There are all kinds of interesting weevils. One species, the Leaf-rolling Beetle, makes a neat little package out of a leaf on which her larva feeds. Another species of weevil lays her eggs in unripe hazel nuts, piercing the soft shell with her mandible so that she can push her egg through the opening. Snugly warm and well fed, the larva develops until the autumn when it pushes its way out of the shell and begins its new life.

The Weevil in the picture lays her eggs in trees, and even the strong, stout trunk of an oak tree is unlikely to defeat a determined Weevil who is searching for a place to deposit her eggs. For this job nature has provided the female Weevil with a snout much longer than the male's.

Weevils come in all shapes and sizes, many of them extremely bizarre, and they form the largest group in the beetle family.

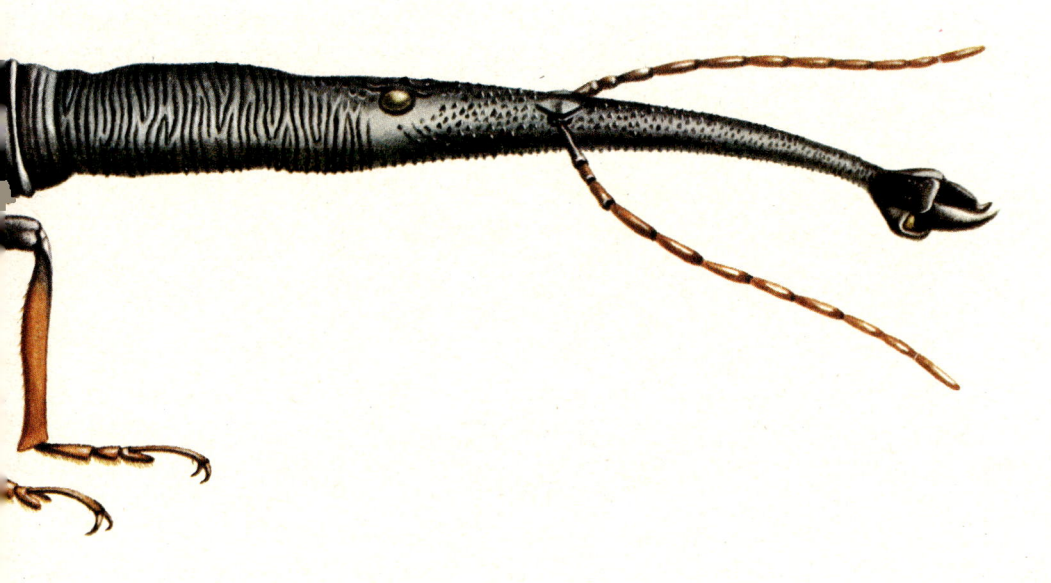

LANTERN FLY

Habitat: South and Central America. **Size:** $2\frac{7}{8}$ in. long; wing-span $5\frac{1}{2}$ in.
It has a head like miniature crocodile jaws.

There are a number of fantastic looking insects found in tropical South America that are known as Lantern Flies. All of them have weird, grotesque growths on their heads that are really hollow tubes.

At one time it was thought, quite wrongly as it turned out, that these insects were luminous and so they were given their somewhat misleading name 'Lantern'.

Lantern Flies belong to the family Fulgoridea and one of the strangest members is the one shown here with its peanut-shaped head growth that suggests the jaws of a crocodile! In contrast to their grotesque heads, Lantern Flies have vivid and very beautiful markings on their hind wings which are visible in flight.

LEAF INSECT

Habitat: Southern Asia and Africa.
Size: Approx. 4 in.
It looks like a leaf.

This insect belongs to the family Phyllidae. So effective is its mimicry that it is hard to say whether you are looking at a leaf or an insect.

Entomologists confirm that this type of insect is so convincingly camouflaged that quite often it is mistakenly bitten by another leaf-eating insect! These intriguing insects that nature has so cunningly camouflaged for their own protection are comparatively rare. This is because they reproduce so slowly—their tiny seed-like eggs taking up to six months to hatch. The females are bigger than the males and have lost their ability to fly. Some of the most fantastic Leaf Insects are found in Southern Asia and Africa. As they rest motionless among the foliage, everything about them—colour, structure and attitude—is superbly staged to deceive the eye.

COMMON STICK INSECT

Habitat: Australia. **Size:** Approx. 5 in.
It looks like a stick.

Like their cousins, the Leaf Insects, Common Stick Insects are wonderful mimics. They look so much like the twigs from which they hang that it is sometimes extraordinarily difficult to see where the insect begins and the twig ends!
Many species are wingless and parthenogenetic. Parthenogenesis is a word used in biology to indicate that the egg can be developed without fertilisation. In other words, female Stick Insects can produce their eggs without any help from the males. However, when this is a common occurrence, usually only females are produced. These insects lead a precarious life, but when they are attacked they can often escape by breaking off one of their legs and leaving it behind, knowing that the abandoned leg will soon be replaced by a new one.

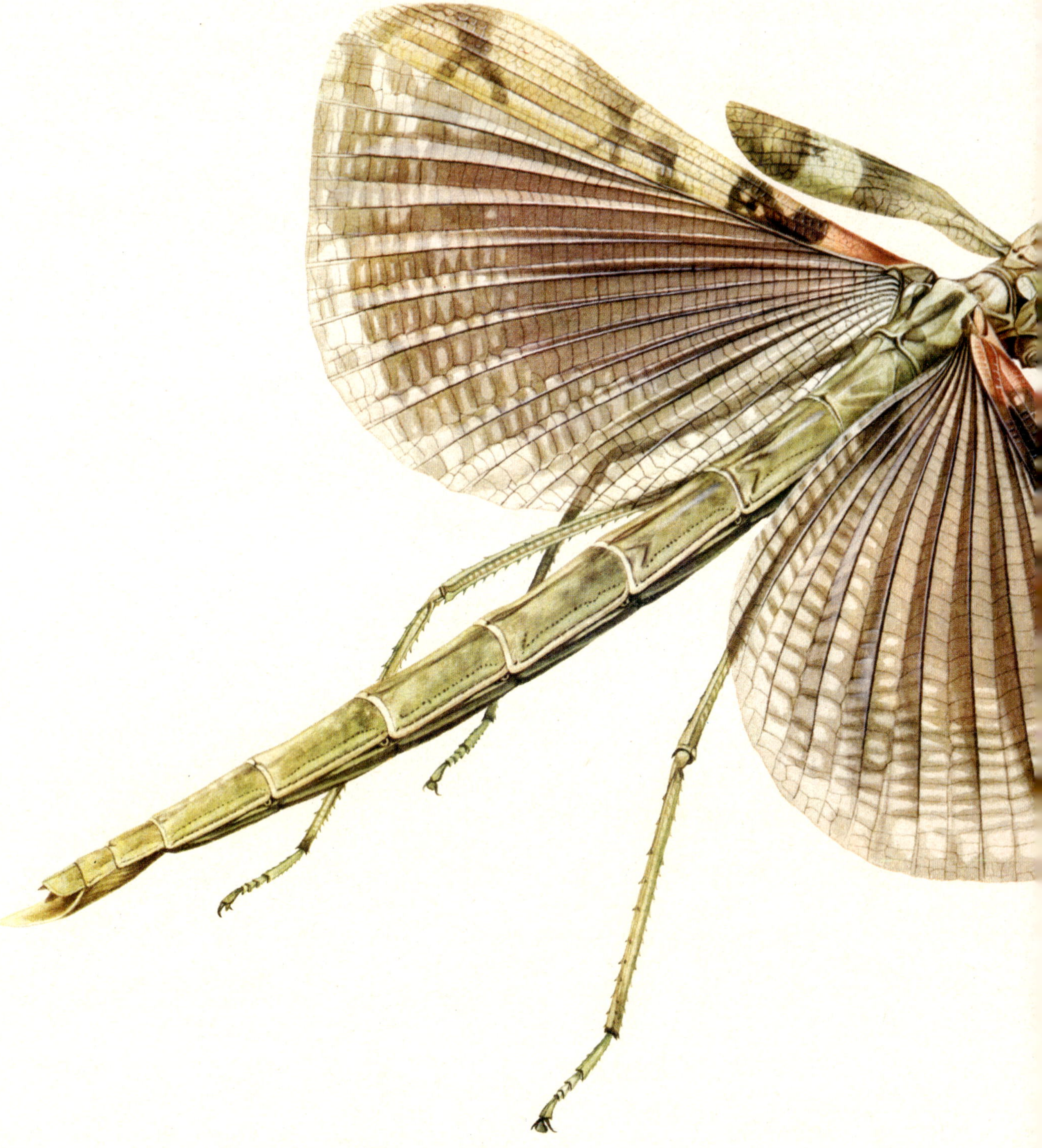

WALKINGSTICK

Habitat: Australia. **Size:** 8½ in., up to 13 in.
It walks like an insect on stilts.

A very close relative indeed to the Stick Insect is the appropriately named Walkingstick. These long-legged insects spend their days hanging motionless from plants until night falls. Then, for all the world looking like insects on stilts, they make their way at a slow pace through the undergrowth and if caught walking or climbing they will eject a pungent smelling liquid at their attacker.
Most stick insects lay tough-skinned eggs that are the size of tiny seeds. The female Walkingstick may deposit as many as a hundred over the course of ten days or so. Then, as if satisfied that she has complied with one of nature's laws, she dies. We read on the previous page how the Common Stick Insects are, for the most part, parthenogenetic and this also applies to the Walkingsticks. There are no males at all in some species. Walkingstick eggs hatch under the protective covering of darkness, but the percentage of losses must be very high for there are numerous lizards, birds, spiders and wasps that consider these larvae appetising snacks.

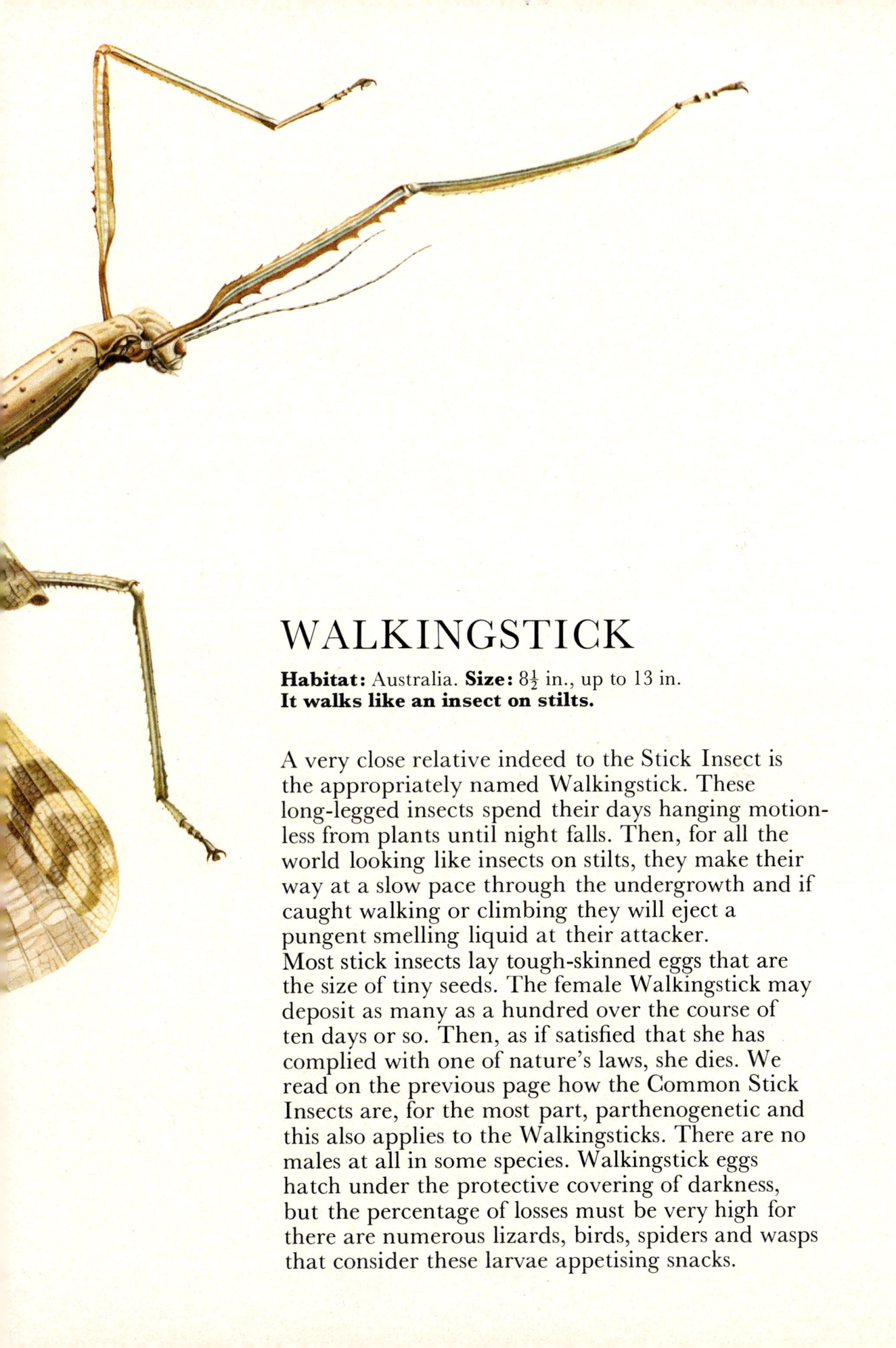

DEATH'S HEAD CICADA

Habitat: Japan and Chinese mainland. **Size:** 3 in.
It has a skull marking.

This odd looking insect is a true member of the singing family Cicadidae. There are several species but nearly all cicadas are found in tropical countries where they live in bushes and trees. It is the male that sings and you can hear his song, loud and shrill, when the sun is at its brightest overhead.
Most singing cicadas have wonderful, transparent wings that glisten in the sunlight.
The Death's Head Cicada shown here has strange skull markings on its back. Not surprisingly, this skull-like design has given rise to many superstitions.

CROESUS MOTH

Habitat: Tropical South America and Africa. **Size:** wing-span $3\frac{1}{2}$ in.
It is one of the most beautiful moths.

Nearly all moths fly about at night, but the exceptionally beautiful Croesus Moth, found in tropical South America and Africa, flies about in the day-time. As it flies, high above the ground, its wings, as the picture suggests, show a wonderful iridescent quality. The brilliant beauty of this moth can really only be appreciated when it is at rest, wings open. Seen in this way, it is considered by many entomologists to be the most beautiful moth in the whole world.
It would not be surprising if many of these entrancing moths were mistaken for butterflies, but when a moth settles it nearly always spreads its wings out flat or folds them over its body. This is something a butterfly never does. When butterflies come to rest they raise their wings upwards and fold them together. Also remember that a butterfly has little knobs on its antennae which the moth does not.

WINDOWPANE BUTTERFLY

Habitat: Amazon Basin in Brazil. **Size:** wing-span 3 in.
It is one of the most beautiful insects.

All the butterflies of the world are beautiful and some, like the Windowpane Butterfly, have a delicate, breathtaking beauty in flight that is not easily forgotten. This one also has two eyes painted on its otherwise transparent wings, which deceive its predators into thinking they are being watched. Some butterflies' eggs may be red or blue but most of them are a greenish colour. When the eggs hatch out, the soft-bodied little caterpillars give no hint of the lovely creatures they will finally become. Many of the tropical species are brilliantly coloured and the caterpillars, too, are sometimes orange, yellowish red and even striped. Strange as it may seem, these strong bright colours actually frighten away their enemies and it is often the perfectly camouflaged brownish-green caterpillars that get eaten by the birds.

DEATH'S HEAD HAWK MOTH

Habitat: Europe and Great Britain. **Size:** 4 in.
It is the largest British moth.

Moths and butterflies belong to the order Lepidoptera, and it would be unfair to look upon moths as the poor relations! Many are extremely beautiful and some, like the Death's Head Hawk Moth, are quite rare.
The Death's Head Hawk Moth, the largest of British moths, owes its strange name to the skull markings on its back which are very similar to those of the Death's Head Cicada, pictured earlier. Size and markings apart, this Hawk Moth is certainly unusual. Most moths are, for the most part, silent, but catch a Death's Head Hawk Moth in your hand and it will give a loud squeak! The majority of the hawk species of moth have very long tongues so that they can suck the nectar out of the flowers, but the honey-loving Death's Head has a very short stiff pointed tongue which it uses to break into bees' honeycombs.
Just like butterflies, moths lay eggs that develop into caterpillars. The Death's Head Hawk Moth caterpillar is large and yellow.

TREEHOPPERS

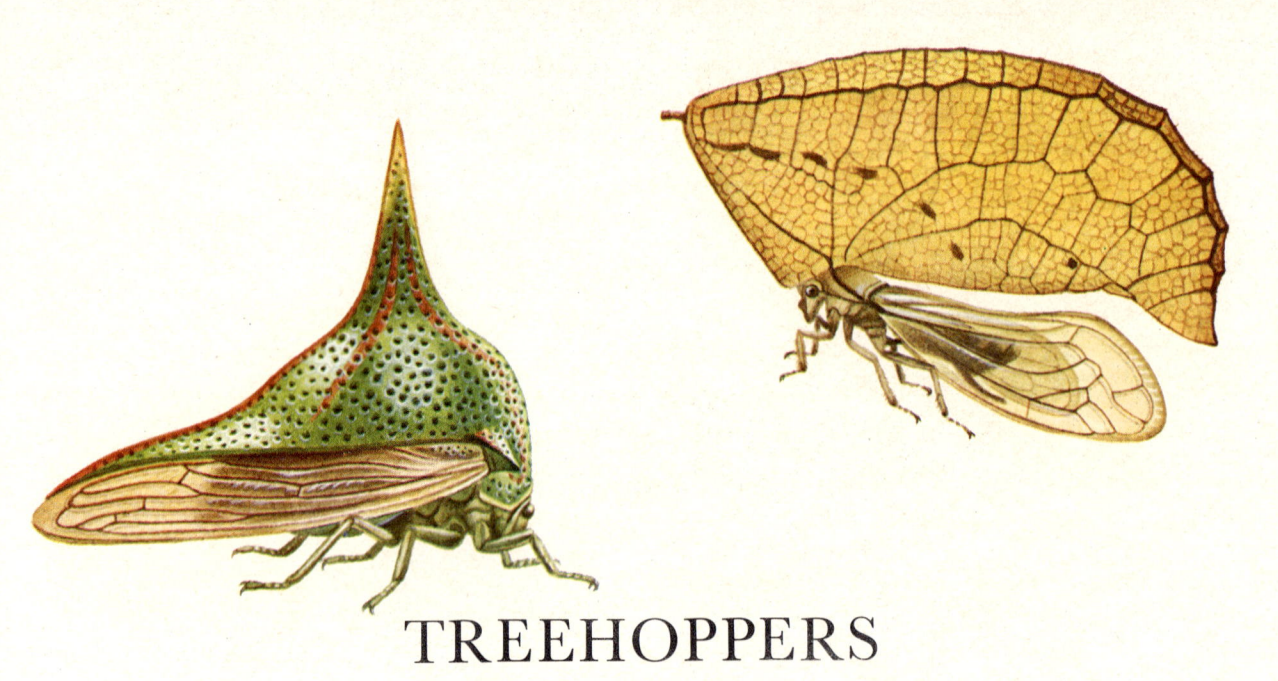

Habitat: Tropics, most in South America. **Size:** less than 1 in. **They have fantastic shapes.**

The athletic little Treehoppers that can run, jump and fly are part of the Cicadine family. They have a most efficient piercing and sucking proboscis by means of which they suck the juices from plants.

There are many species of Treehoppers and, as you can see from the pictures, they all have extraordinary, eye-catching growths. Many of the most fantastic of these insects live in South America where they do a great deal of damage to crops and fruit trees.
Many female Treehoppers have long sharp ovipositors so that they can lay their eggs in the bark of twigs. The nymphs look rather like miniature cockscombs. Entomologists cannot explain why Treehoppers have such deforming and spectacular outgrowths. So dwarfed and hidden are the bodies of the insects that it is impossible to say exactly what shape they really are. Certainly, the Treehoppers themselves, unlike the Stick Insects and the Mantids, do not seem to be particularly bothered whether or not their curved, bent or flattened projections match their immediate surroundings!

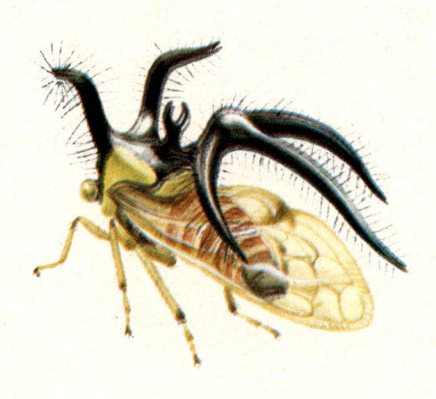

WAXEN-TAILED PLANTHOPPER

Habitat: World-wide. **Size:** 2⅛ in.
It has a tail of wax.

Like treehoppers, planthoppers also have sucking mouth parts. There are a great number of different species of this insect scattered through the world and they are generally considered to be destructive pests by farmers and fruit growers.

Many planthoppers secrete a sugary liquid that ants and other insects find quite irresistible. Others, like the Waxen-tailed Planthopper you see here, have fantastic ribbon-like tails of wax that drop off from time to time and are confiscated by a certain species of moth caterpillar as food.

Butterflies are often considered to be among the most beautiful insects in the world, but some of the large glassy-winged, tropical planthoppers frequently rival the butterfly in their exotic beauty.

LEAF-FOOTED BUG

Habitat: South America. **Size:** $\frac{7}{8}$ in.
It has leaf-like feet.

Most of us are reluctant to think about bugs because their dictionary definition is evil-smelling and bed-infesting! But there is a large group of colourful, fascinating bugs that bears little resemblance in appearance to the bugs everybody fears!
Many members of the True Bug family have fantastic extensions and back decorations that make them extremely interesting.
The tiny Leaf-footed Bug in the picture is found in South America where it feeds on tomatoes and other fruits, extracting the juice by sucking. Its vivid colour and attractive appearance belies its destructive habits! Bugs are found in most parts of the world, being able to survive in quite rigorous climates.
Some species make excellent mothers, covering up their eggs when it begins to rain, whilst one species of female Leaf-footed Bug actually turns her husband into an egg-bearer by gluing her eggs on to his back!

MANTIS

Habitat: India. **Size:** 3½ in.
It looks like a violin.

Ferocious yet seemingly prayerful in repose, the mantids of the insect kingdom are, humanly speaking, creatures of cruel cunning with insatiable appetites!

Master-hands at mimicry, mantids may take on the guise of a twig or a flower so effectively that other insects never suspect their presence until they find themselves grasped between a pair of powerful spiny legs from which there is no escape. But it is the female of the species that attracts our reluctant admiration for, at certain times, she thinks nothing of devouring her husband, head first!

There are about 2,000 different species of mantids. The Mantis shown here on the left lives in India and, because of its shape, it is commonly known as the 'Wandering Violin'. Most mantids rely upon their colour and markings, not only to hide them from their victims, but also from their enemies. If the African Mantis pictured below is disturbed, it opens its wings and flashes its startling 'eyes' to scare off its attacker.

Some mantids are greenish-brown, the colour of the leaves and twigs on which they sit. There they wait, motionless, until their next victim comes along.

MANTIS

Habitat: Africa. **Size:** $1\frac{1}{2}$ in.
It has 'eyes' on its wings.

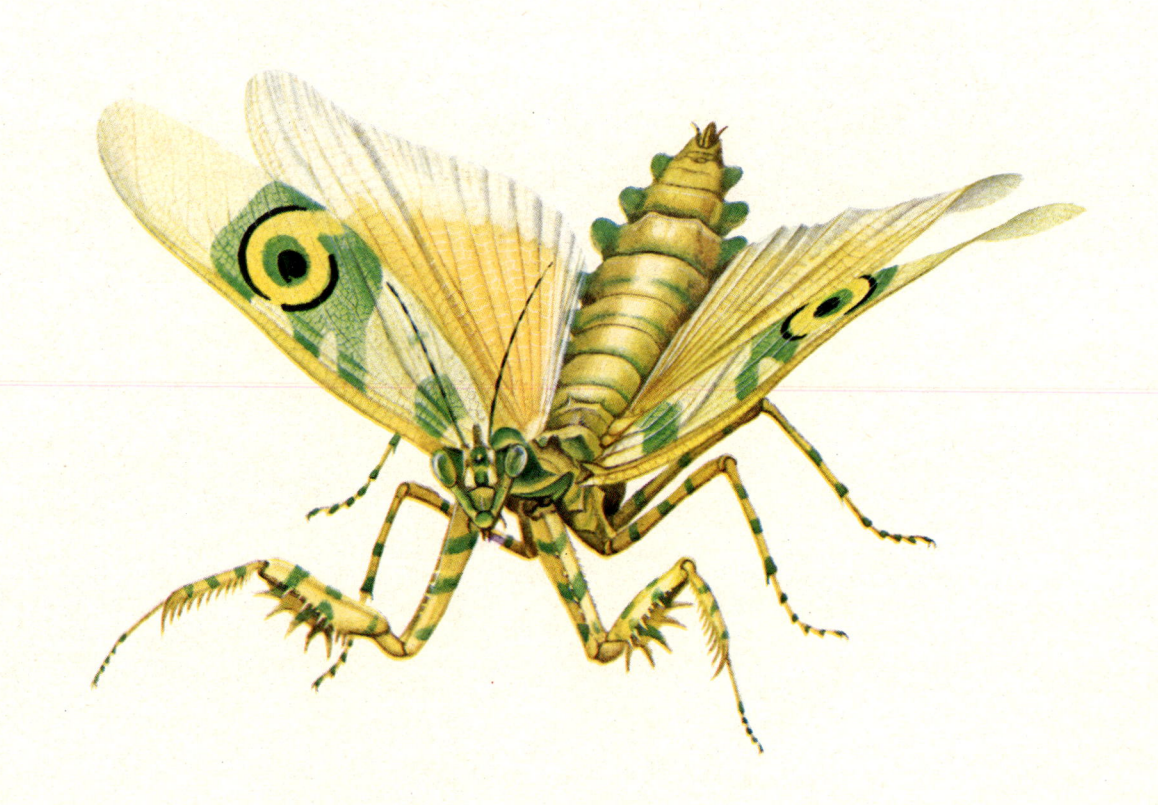

FALSE LEAF BUSH CRICKET

Habitat: South America. **Size:** 2¼ in.
It is fantastically camouflaged.

Bush crickets—or katydids as they are often called—form a group called the 'Long-horned Grasshoppers'. The False Leaf Katydid, with its long antennae, is a typical example of nature at her best when it comes to camouflage. The green colouring and arrangement of veins on its wings provide a perfect disguise for this leaf insect. It is so well camouflaged that you would have to look twice if you wanted to spot it among the foliage.

Insects have many ways of preserving their lives but by far the greatest number of them like the False Leaf Katydid, rely on camouflage. To make this supremely effective, the False Leaf Katydid chooses a leaf which, in colouring and texture, closely resembles itself. Entomologists call this type of camouflage 'cryptic garb'. We can find many examples of this in the insect world.

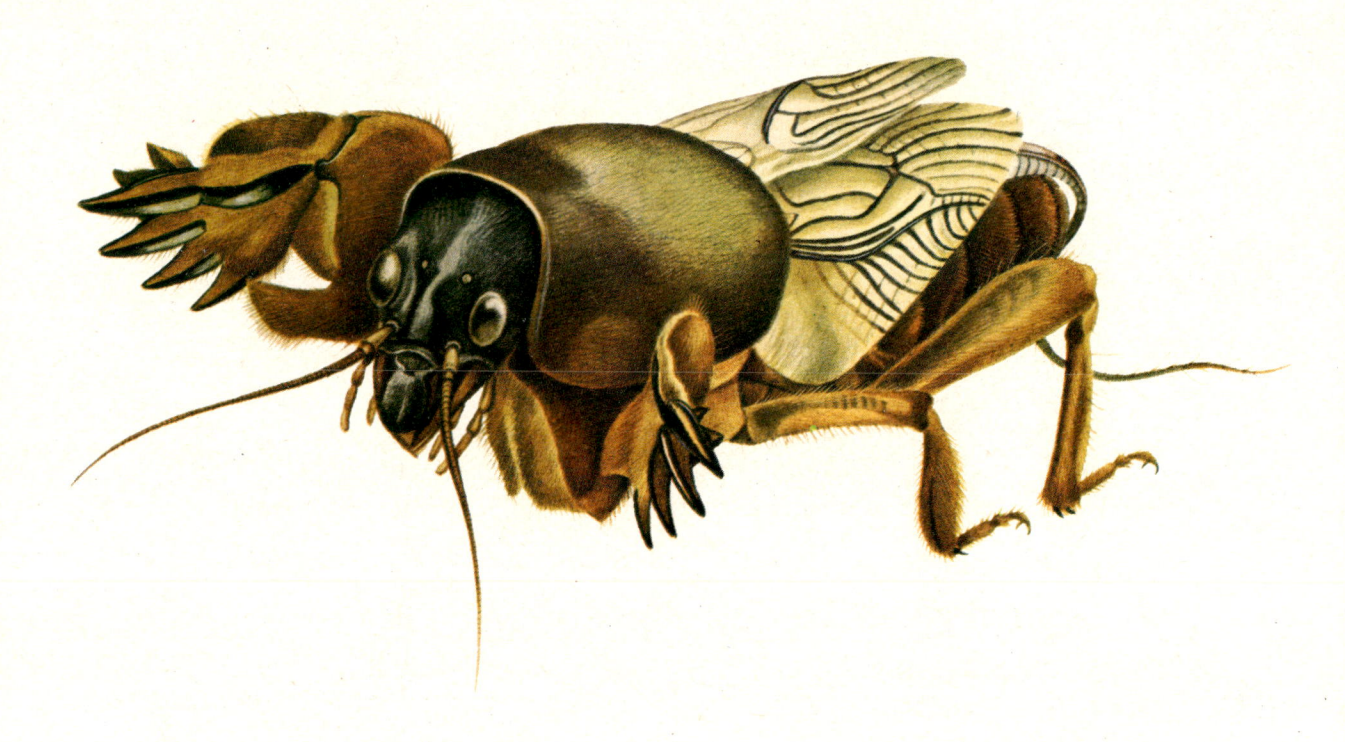

MOLE-CRICKET

Habitat: Europe. **Size:** 1½–2 in.
It burrows like a mole.

One of the most interesting members of the cricket family is the stout, energetic Mole-cricket, the biggest of all the crickets found in Europe.
The Mole-cricket has a front pair of spade-like legs, similar to those of the mole. With these it burrows into the earth where, for the most part, it lives. In the spring, the female Mole-cricket deposits her eggs, sometimes as many as 300, in a cosy underground nesting chamber. The larvae remain there for between two to three years developing into adults. Although the larvae take so long to mature, the Mole-cricket's own life, barring accidents, lasts only a year.
If you have been lucky enough to see a Mole-cricket at dusk, you may have observed its large, transparent wings as it flies low over the grass. And perhaps, too, you have heard the male's purring, staccato song that it sings when it is out to attract a mate.
The Mole-cricket's song is quite different from the field cricket's strident chirp. We talk about crickets' songs, but to be more exact, the 'musical' notes we hear are made by certain parts of their forewings rubbing together.

GRASSHOPPER

Habitat: India.
Size: Head to tip of abdomen, *male:* up to 2 in., *female:* up to 2¾ in.
It is one of the best-known 'singing' insects.

This species of Short-horned Grasshopper claims an extremely close relationship to the notorious locust. And, like their cousins, they have enormous appetites.

The Short-Horned Grasshoppers produce their unique, rasping, rattling songs by rubbing their hind legs against their forewings and, like the crickets, they vary their song according to circumstances!

Most species are spectacular jumpers and before finally taking off they seem to sway, rather like an Olympic medallist out to beat his own high-jumping record.

Have you ever seen a grasshopper give itself a wash and brush-up? Just like a kitten, it begins by wetting its face with saliva and then, instead of using its feet as a towel, it bends its head and dries it on the ground.

Like so many of the insects we have read about in this book, grasshoppers rely on camouflage to survive. Still, the odds seem somewhat against them for all kinds of birds, reptiles and other creatures find the noisy, entertaining grasshoppers a very tasty dish!

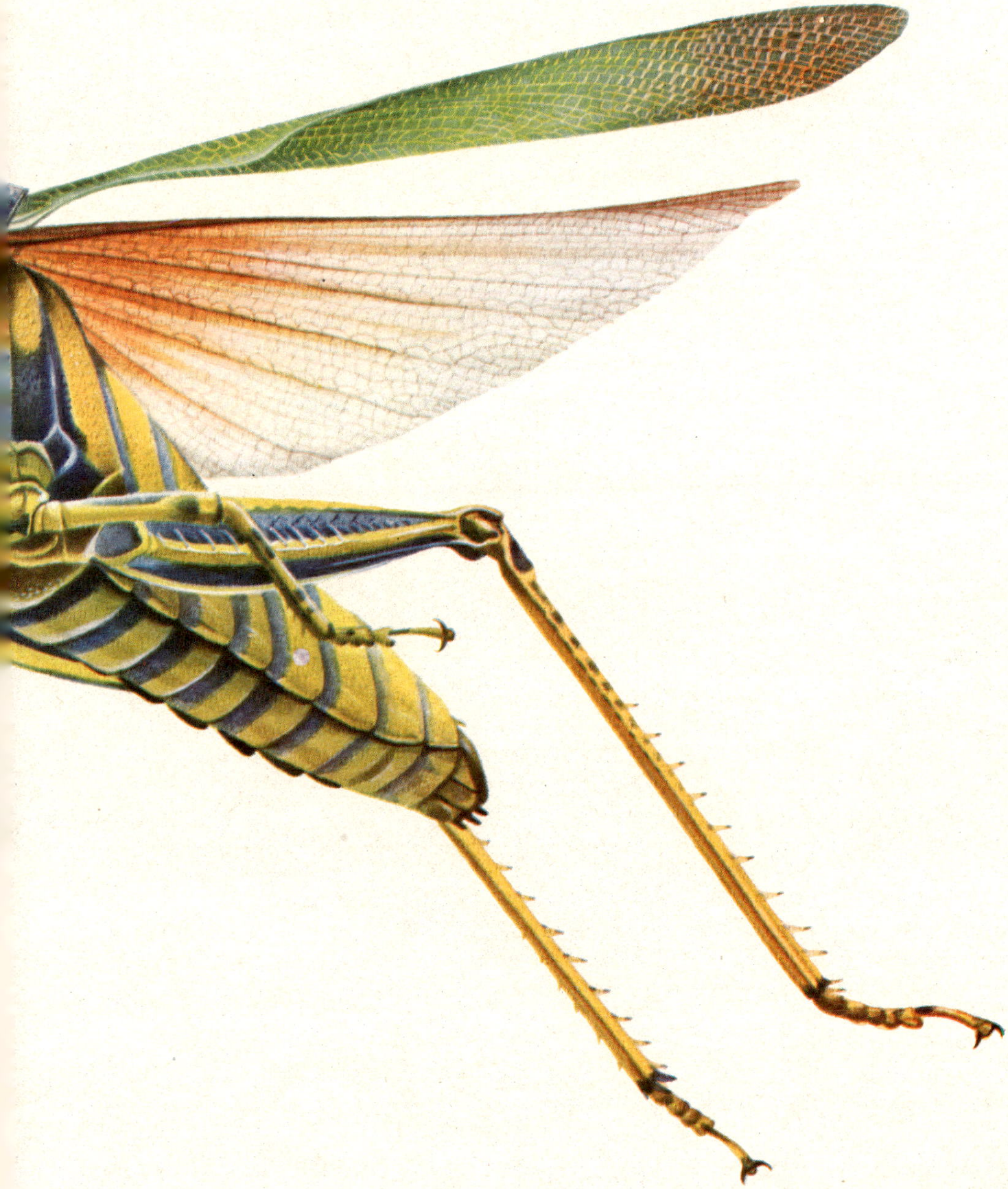

GLOSSARY

abdomen: belly, including the stomach and other organs.

antennae: feelers found on the head of an insect which are used to smell and probe.

cryptic garb: when an insect imitates its environment in colour, texture or movement.

entomology: the study of insects.

grub: an insect larva.

larva: an intermediate stage in insect development, see 'metamorphosis'.

mandibles: the upper pair of jaws.

metamorphosis: the development of an insect from an egg to a larva to a pupa to an adult.

mimicry: when an insect imitates something else, a leaf or twig for example.

nymph: an insect which is not completely developed.

ovipositor: the pointed tube-like organ which a female insect uses to deposit her eggs.

palaentology: the study of ancient forms of life.

parasite: an insect (or plant or animal) which lives in or upon another, drawing food directly from it.

parthenogenesis: reproduction without mating.

proboscis: the elongated part of an insect's mouth.

thorax: the part of the insect's body between the neck and the abdomen or tail.

Planned and directed by The Archon Press Limited, 14-18 Ham Yard, London W1
First published 1975 by Octopus Books Limited, 59 Grosvenor Street, London W1

ISBN 0 7064 0334 7

© 1974 The Archon Press Ltd

Distributed in Australia by Rigby Limited
30 North Terrace, Kent Town, Adelaide, South Australia 5067

Printed in Italy
by Stabilimento Grafico Editoriale
Fratelli Spada - Ciampino-Roma